Geissiane Aguiar

Artificial Intelligence

Geissiane Aguiar

Artificial Intelligence

Mobile robotics applied to artificial neural networks

ScienciaScripts

Imprint
Any brand names and product names mentioned in this book are subject to trademark, brand or patent protection and are trademarks or registered trademarks of their respective holders. The use of brand names, product names, common names, trade names, product descriptions etc. even without a particular marking in this work is in no way to be construed to mean that such names may be regarded as unrestricted in respect of trademark and brand protection legislation and could thus be used by anyone.

Cover image: www.ingimage.com

This book is a translation from the original published under ISBN 978-3-330-99561-1.

Publisher:
Sciencia Scripts
is a trademark of
Dodo Books Indian Ocean Ltd. and OmniScriptum S.R.L publishing group

120 High Road, East Finchley, London, N2 9ED, United Kingdom
Str. Armeneasca 28/1, office 1, Chisinau MD-2012, Republic of Moldova, Europe
Managing Directors: Ieva Konstantinova, Victoria Ursu
info@omniscriptum.com

Printed at: see last page
ISBN: 978-620-8-58212-8

"If knowledge can create problems, it is not through ignorance that we can solve them. ".

Isaac Asimov

To all those who have been and are close to me in some way, making this life ever more worthwhile.

ACKNOWLEDGEMENTS

I was born a sister. The youngest daughter, I came into the world as the youngest, sister to Jussara, the sugar one, and Janderson, the eldest. And so we grew up, between board games, shared secrets, memories - good and bad - shared, fights of rolling on the floor between slaps and long hugs as far as the eye can see - in the beautiful times, in the difficult times, in the singular times when only a long hug realises the size of the joy, or the size of the pain. Without them I wouldn't be half of what I am.

And before I could be a sister, I had to be a daughter. And I fell into the lap of two incredible people who looked after me when I was still helpless and small. José Vianelo and Maria Aparecida are proof that to be a father it's not enough to have children, you have to nurture them with your best so that they germinate and spread good pollen in other fields.

And the days when I find myself weak, I look away and recognise the face of the strongest, most powerful woman I've ever met. A woman who fights silent battles, - tearing her body and soul apart for the love of her family, always raising her face and her scarred body proudly for the world to see. Maria Beloni das Neves is the most powerful warrior who shows me every day that it's necessary to face rough seas in order to become a good sailor.

In the midst of daily battles and high tides, it's always necessary to have someone by your side, to accompany you and understand you, to be your best friend and companion. Lucas Magalhães Ferreira de Carvalho is the person who helps me breathe when things aren't going well, teaching me to be more patient and understanding, helping me navigate a blue that goes beyond colour blindness and beetles.

Transcendent chaos becomes easier when it is shared. Daiane Fontoura and Reinaldo Cicarone are bearers of the washed soul and exposed face who turn my reality into a source of learning, but fight so that the fantasy doesn't disappear. Because really, Carry View and Post Plant are the existence and result of pure imagination that one day became reality. Seeing them, crazy and saintly, silly and serious, children and old people, I'll never forget that "normality" is an imbecilic and sterile illusion.

To get to the top, you have to go through long and thorny paths. And there are always people willing to pass on their knowledge and experience, knowing how to support me through all my academic and personal difficulties. The many professors, especially Everaldo Ribeiro here, were the ones who invited me to fly in their wisdom, even though I knew that flying would depend on my wings.

Life allows us to meet great people with great thoughts.

Edmara Caetano and Francisco Araújo helped me learn that we just need to believe and open our eyes to visualise the best things and those who do us so well, learning that the important thing is not to win, but to go after our dreams, however difficult it may be to obtain them.

If you're lucky, that's how it always ends. And it starts again.

SUMMARY

A new form of interaction and communication is becoming increasingly possible and real through the resources of Artificial Intelligence. Sophisticated computer programmes and specifically chosen hardware make up robots that can even understand human beings in a coherent way. Neural networks have the ability to create fast and effective processing in the human brain.

It provides the knowledge base for various decision-making processes. Nowadays, as is common knowledge, physical or virtual robots have been able to experience the evolution of the human brain, and thus have the ability to reason in a similar way to their progenitors, creating an interface between man and machine.

In this way, man, who has had the unique capacity for reasoning for thousands of years, is affected by the field of artificial intelligence, which goes beyond building intelligent entities to help us with tasks and carry out work. This work has the intuition to study and build intelligent platforms for the most diverse uses, capable of understanding and assisting in tasks and/or positioning. Through communication between a robot and an elderly or disabled person, it is possible to meet the needs of everyday life in various areas, enabling much more than socialising and entertainment.

KEYWORDS: Robotics, Artificial Intelligence, Mobile Robotics.

SUMMARY

INTRODUCTION

Artificial intelligence is a recent science, encompassing a huge variety of sub-fields, from areas of general use, such as learning and perception, to specific tasks. Artificial intelligence systematises and automates intellectual tasks and is therefore potentially relevant to any option of human intellectual activity.

From reality to fiction, we can see the presence of artificial intelligence in robots, such as the maid Rosie from "The Jetsons"; the robots from "Lost in Space"; "I, Robot" by author Isaac Asimov, the robot-human from "Artificial Intelligence", the robots from the "Star Wars" series; the "NAO" robot used to teach children how to programme; "Pepper" the gentle and lovable emotional robot and even "Watson", a robot who took part in a reality quiz show and even won a job at a certain Brazilian bank.

With various technologies and advances in them, man, who has had the unique ability to think for thousands of years, is proving that artificial intelligence goes beyond building intelligent entities to questioning whether machines can really think and how far their functionality can be improved.

The main objective of this work is to understand how artificial intelligence works, studying the use of artificial neural networks and logical reasoning applications in mobile robotics. It also aims to analyse mobile robotics in order to improve reasoning applications using intelligent systems, studying the "brain" of robots and their way of making logical decisions, as well as their thinking and behaviour.

The methodologies used were qualitative and quantitative, analysing data based on a bibliographical review, documentary analysis and sporadic studies on the subject.

In the first chapter, we have an introduction and concept of Artificial Intelligence, analysing its history in the world and evolution up to the present day being applied in intelligent systems in various areas of research.

The second chapter covers neural networks, both biological and artificial, their functions and an introduction to neurocomputing, which is used to assimilate a human brain.

In the third chapter, we were able to grasp the history and main functionality of robotics in general, its usability and benefits for society. In this same chapter, we were also able to differentiate between robot classifications and the mobile robotics in question.

The fourth chapter provides a simple overview of the ease of use of robotics applied to artificial neural networks, as well as their operating logic, main benefits and use.

CHAPTER 1

CONCEPT OF ARTIFICIAL INTELLIGENCE

Artificial Intelligence (AI) is a branch of computing that involves designing devices that simulate the human capacity to reason, perceive, make decisions and solve problems, in short, the capacity to be intelligent.

Having existed for decades, this area of science has been strongly boosted by the rapid development of information technology and computing, causing new elements to be rapidly added to AI.

1.1 Historical Introduction to Artificial Intelligence

Beginning in the 1940s, research into this new science was carried out only to find new functions for the computer, which was still in the design stage. With the outbreak of the Second World War, there was also a need to develop technology to boost the arms industry.

Over time, broad lines of study in AI have emerged, one of which is biological, which studies the development of concepts that aim to imitate human neural networks. In the 1960s, this science was called Artificial Intelligence and researchers in the biological field believed that machines could carry out complex human tasks and reason.

Studies on neural networks only returned to the fore in the 1980s, with the construction and study of a training algorithm called backpropagation, based on the back propagation of errors to make adjustments to the weights in the intermediate layers. This success led to other research based on artificial neural networks and a variety of cognitive models, but it was in 1999 that it was given a major boost, truly consolidating Artificial Intelligence studies.

1.2 Intelligent Systems Applications

Artificial Intelligence is already present in people's daily lives. According to Figure 1, AI can be applied to various areas of activity. For example, in the development of games, which use this study as a basis for creating new, increasingly complex games. Another example is cameras that automatically focus on people's faces or shoot when they see a smile. Even word processors' spell checkers need an intelligent system to detect a syntax problem in a sentence and offer a possible correction.

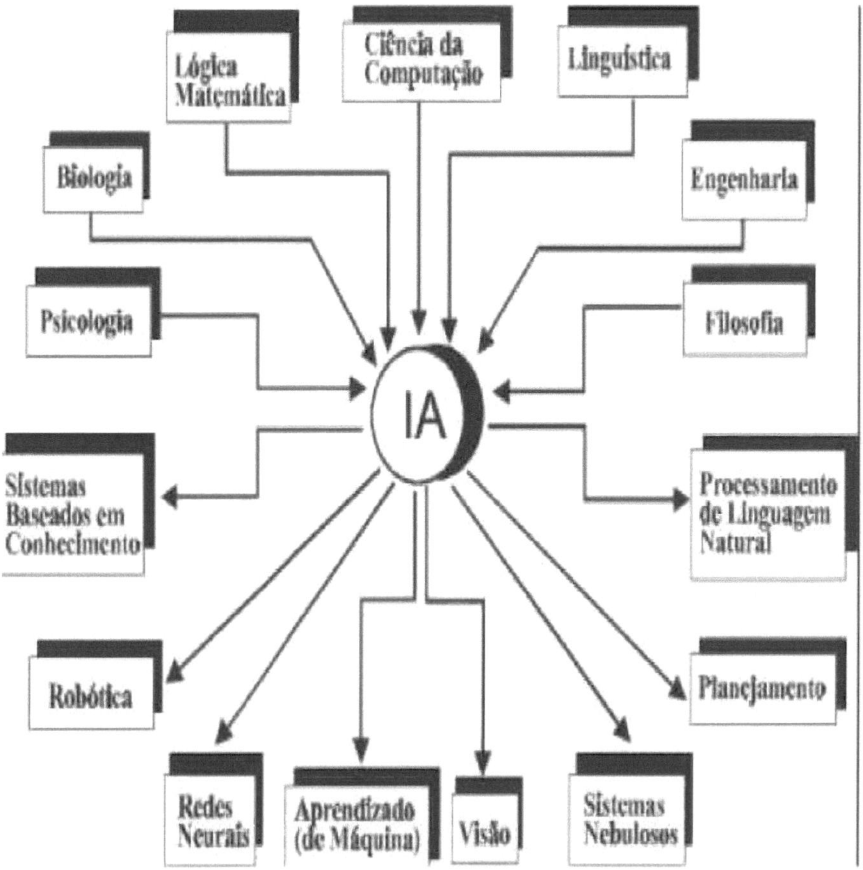

Figure 1 - Areas related to Artificial Intelligence
Source: Wikipedia.

Medicine is full of machines with Artificial Intelligence applications, there are instruments, for example, that in addition to detecting the patient's problem are able to determine the best treatment for him.

Heckerman (1991) describes a case in which a specialist in lymph node pathology ridiculed a programme's diagnosis in a particularly difficult case. The machine's creators then suggested that he ask the computer for an explanation of the diagnosis, thus highlighting the main factors that influenced its decision and the interaction of various symptoms in this case, so that the expert ended up agreeing with the system.

CHAPTER 2

NEURAL NETWORKS

Humans have developed machines to help us with everyday tasks, improving our labour, time and strength. Rarely do you find a machine that does something a human being can't do, but they all do it in a more competent way.

According to studies by Guilherme Paraol (2011), with computerisation at work, researchers ended up developing machines capable of helping us think.

Despite the defence that intelligence is the fruit of logical thinking, a number of different logical systems have been developed, resulting in the creation of computers. For others, human intelligence is the result of how well structured and organised the brain is.

With the creation of the theory of Neural Networks, which took place around 1940 and 1950, due to the fact that they were such promising networks to study, several researchers thought that this model would never reach the emphasis of logical computing known and used today, however, with the advance of neuroscience, research into neural networks has been well developed, but for this, it is necessary to know how neurons work.

1.3 The Biological Neurone

According to Feldman (2007), neurons are the cells that make up our brain. They have three main parts, as shown in Figure 2.

- Dentrites: Responsible for capturing information or the environment and/or other mobiles.
- The cellular body or Soma: Responsible for processing information.
- Axon: Distributes processed information to other neurons or body cells.

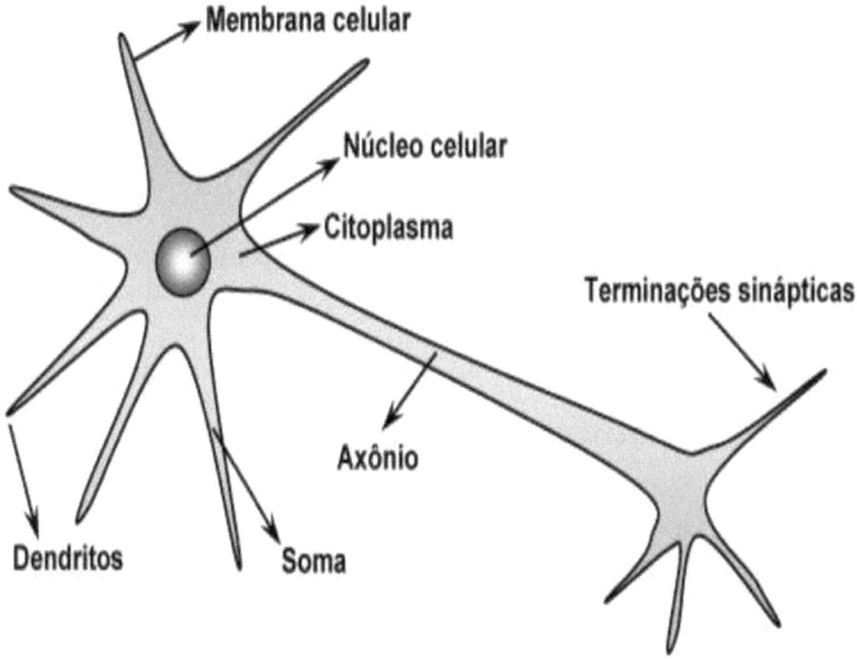

Figure 2 - Biological neuron

Source: Book Introduction to Psychology, FELDMAN (2007)

Most of the time, cells work alone. The more they work together, the more they become capable of

processing, which is why several neurons are needed to obtain the best performance.

The human brain is considered to be the most impressive carbon-based processor in existence. It is made up of around ten billion neurons, which are responsible for all the functions and movements of the organism and, being connected, form a large network called the neural network, conducting stimuli through concentrations of Na+ (Sodium) and K+ (Potassium), achieving great capacity for processing and storing information.

Their communication is carried out by means of impulses, which, when received, are processed and given an action threshold, triggering a second impulse that is received, triggering another impulse that produces a neurotransmitter substance which flows from the cell body to the axon.

These neural networks do not transmit negative signals, they are uniform in some parts of the body and have asynchronous pulses due to the fact that they are not continuous.

1.4 The Artificial Neurone

Dating back to the first information on neurocomputing in 1943, the articles by McCulloch & Pitts suggested building a machine based on or inspired by the human brain. In this suggestion, each neuron could be implemented as shown in figure 3.

In 1949, Donald Hebb wrote a book entitled "The *Organisation of Beahvior"*, which put forward the idea that psychological conditioning was present in any part of animals due to the fact this is a property of individual neurons, and which later served to develop new research based on a specific learning law for the synapses of neurons.

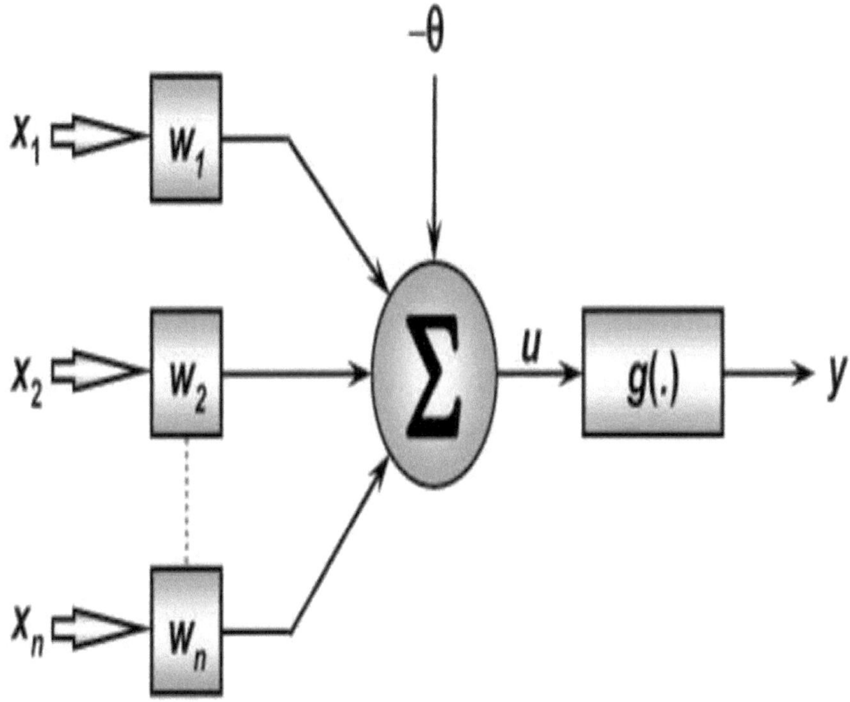

Figure 3 - The simplest artificial neuron model was proposed in 1943 by McCulloch & Pitts.

Source: A logical calculus of the ideas immanent in nervous activity. Bulletin of Mathematical Biophysics, University of Oxford, MCCULLOCH & PITTS (1943)

During this period, the first neurocomputer was built, the so-called Snark, by Mavin Minsky, in the year 1951; operating successfully from a technical starting point, adjusting its weights automatically, however, it never performed any interesting information processing functions.

In 1956, two branches of Artificial Intelligence were born: symbolic and connectionist.

Symbolic Artificial Intelligence tries to simulate human intelligent behaviour by disregarding the mechanisms responsible for it. Connectionist Artificial Intelligence believes that by building a system that simulates the structure of the brain, this system will exhibit intelligence, i.e. it will be able to learn, assimilate, make mistakes and learn from its mistakes.

The first successful neurocomputer (Mark I Perceptron) appeared between 1957 and 1958, created by Frank Rosenblatt, Charles Wightman and others, which revolutionised the modern way of thinking with its technical contributions, and is seen as the founder of neurocomputing.

Bernard Widrow, with the help of his graduate student Ted Hoff, developed a new type of neural network processing element called the Adaline, which is still in use today (unlike the Perceptron).

The following years were marked by an exaggerated enthusiasm on the part of many researchers in the field, which caused - with the publication of many articles and books - an unreliable forecast for the time.

Between 1967 and 1982, there was a period of silent research when little research was published.

Courage embraced researchers in the 1980s, when they published various proposals to explore the development of neural networks and their applications. A very important fact was that Ira Skurnick, a programme manager at DARPA (Defence Advanced Research Agency) decided to listen to the various researches and arguments, founding neurocomputing research in 1983, giving DARPA the status of one of the world leaders when it came to technological "fashion".

John Hopfield, a world-renowned physicist, became interested in neurocomputing and wrote articles used by many professionals in the field.

With the publication of the book "Parallel Distributed *Processing*", edited by David Rumelhart and James McClelland, the field of research exploded with the first conference on neural networks, held in 1987 in San Francisco; the IEEE International Conference on Neural Networks, and the International Neural Networks Society (INSS) was also formed, followed by the foundation of the INSS journal in 1989, Neural Computation and the IEEE Transactions on Neural Networks in 1990.

1.4.1 Neurocomputing and its motivations

The main function of the neural model is to process similarly to the brain, so neural networks are responsible for approximating the structure of the brain to that of an ordinary modern computer, where information is transferred at set times within a relationship with a synchronised signal.

Following man's discovery of machines, there was a desire to create machines that could be independent of human intervention in order to operate, being able to learn and interact with previously unknown environments.

The main motivation for developing and researching these machines was human organisms, which provide different ways of learning algorithms and adapting. In this way, it is hoped that some of the characteristics present in biological organisms and their adaptations will be similar to machine learning.

The difference between the machine and the human brain is that the latter works in parallel, being extremely connected and more efficient at solving tasks that have several variations.

Machines inspired by biology base their processing on mathematical models, which is why machines inspired by biology are different from today's machines.

CHAPTER 3

ROBOTICS

In a nutshell, robotics is a technological science that includes areas such as mechanics, electronics, computing; composing systems made up of machines, mechanical parts and integrated circuits.

To a lesser extent, microelectronics, artificial intelligence, human factors and production engineering also make up various branches of robotics.

3.1 Historical Introduction to Robots

Leonardo Da Vinci is said to have designed the first humanoid robot in history in 1945, depicting a mechanical knight apparently capable of moving his arms, head and jaw.

With the writing of Electric Man by Luis Senarens in 1885, various robotic inspirations emerged, serving only as inspiration, because until then they were fictional works and very little could be built.

Shiroma's (2004) studies show that Tortoise, considered one of the first mobile robots, was built by W. Grey Walter in 1950. Tortoise was able to follow light sources and dodge obstacles.

In 1956, George Devil and Joseph Engelberger opened the world's first robot factory called Unimation, a manufacturer of Puma manipulator arms (figure 4).

Figure 4 - Puma robotic arm in 1961. Source: Engelberger Establishes Unimation, Inc.

Widesoft (2006) writes that in 1952, Bell Laboratories made the development of electronics feasible with the invention of transistors, a basic component in the construction of computers, thus breaking several restrictions on the development of robotics.

Between 1958 and 1959, Robert Noyce, Jean Hoerni, Jack Kilby and Kurt Lehovec developed the first integrated circuit (IC) - which is now known as a chip, incorporating several dozen transistors already interconnected on a single very small chip, thus making electronic circuits more complex.

With the advance of these technologies, artificial intelligence has developed with the same intensity and speed. John McCarthy defined it in a popular way by introducing the following statement at the famous Dartmouth conference in 1956: "Make a machine behave in such a way that it would be called intelligent if it were the behaviour of a human being".

According to Arkin (1998), in order to learn about robotics, robots must be built, because when working only with theory based on simulations, many details are lost. The construction of robots was restricted in the 1960s and 1970s, so all the robots that emerged at that time were noted in the cybernetic evolution.

Nilsson (1969) understands and reports that Sharkey was a robot built at the Stanford Research Institute at the end of the 60s. This robot was capable of sensing and modelling the environment around it, planning trajectories and carrying out programmed actions via a computer.

Hillare, a robot built in 1977 by the Laboratory of Automation and Systems Analysis (LAAS) in Toulose, France - weighed 400kg and was equipped with three wheels, a computer vision system, ultrasonic sensors and laser distance detectors. Hillare could move around autonomously as described by Giralt (1984) in his book.

Last but not least, a robotic platform was built and used by Moravec to test navigation using a stereo vision system (figure 5). This system was called the Stanford Cart and described by Moravec himself (1977).

Figure 5 - Hans Moravec with the Stanford Cart in 1977.

Source: Obstacle avoidance and navigation in the real world by a seeing robot rover, MORAVEC (1977).

In order to explore Mars, NASA (2003) built two geological robots called Opportunity and Spirit (figure 6), which landed on Mars on 8 and 25 July 2004, respectively. These robots were developed with the main aim of sending back images, as well as analysing rocks and craters, looking for signs of the possible existence of water on the planet.

Figure 6 - Spirit and Opportunity on their mission to Mars in 2004.

Source: NASA (2003).

Later, the Massachusetts Artificial Intelligence Laboratory

(MIT) developed the adorable Cog, a robot capable of interacting with humans and learning like a child (figure 7). Cog ended up realising two theories: that a robot could learn and that interactions would be more natural the more "human" a robot looked. With sensors, cameras and 22 degrees of movement, it became the first humanoid with cognitive development.

Figure 7 - Cog robot and one of its creators at the Massachusetts Institute of Technology (MIT).

Source: Massachusetts Institute of Technology (MIT).

3.1.1 Robot classification

There are three classes of robot:

- Industrial;
- Doctors and;
- Furniture.

Industrial robots are the most widespread in economic tasks. They are made up of an articulated structure that moves and adapts to different configurations according to orders received from a control unit that is usually based on a microprocessor.

Medical, co-operation or rehabilitation robots are designed as intelligent prostheses for people with special physical needs that differ from the rest in their shape, which seeks to have the appearance of the corresponding human extremity, to perform its functions and that the signals emitted come from nerve or muscle signals.

These prostheses can bend the elbow, rotate the wrist or move the shoulder. They can imitate some 25 of the 30 movements developed by a human arm, allowing people to pick up small objects such as sultanas and even a glass of water.

This category also includes robots specifically developed as assistants in surgical tasks of great precision or high complexity, such as the Da Vinci surgical robot at Saint Clare's Hospital in Denville (USA). This system is unique in the world and will enable major advances to be made in less invasive surgery, using cutting-edge surgical instruments and three-dimensional (3D) visualisation systems.

Mobile robots are automatic transport devices, i.e. they are mechanical platforms equipped with a locomotion system capable of navigating through a given working environment, equipped with a certain level of autonomy for their locomotion and carrying loads. Their applications can be very varied and are always related to tasks that are usually risky or harmful to human health, in areas such as agriculture, in the transport of dangerous cargo or in solitary or co-operative exploration tasks with other unmanned vehicles. Classic examples are the transport and collection of materials, nuclear reactor maintenance tasks, the handling of explosive materials, underground exploration, etc.

It is necessary to clarify that the concept of autonomy is not only related to energy issues, but also refers to the ability to perceive, model, plan and act to achieve certain objectives, without the intervention (or with very little intervention) of the human operator, since the robot can move around in structured or unstructured environments, totally or partially known. The human operator's role must be played by the vehicle's own control system, which must supply it with the intelligence needed to make it move correctly.

The name mobile robot refers to this ability to achieve one or more objectives with very little intervention from human supervisors. On the other hand, the term self-guided vehicle refers to mobile structures that only follow pre-established paths (lines painted on the ground, magnetic strips, reflective strips).

3.2 Mobile Robotics

A mobile robot is an automatic device capable of performing movements and interacting in a defined environment. Their main purpose is to have a sufficient level of autonomy to be able to interact with the world in which they carry out their tasks.

This multidisciplinary research area means that microelectronics, computer science, mechanics and control systems work together to improve the learning of these robots. As such, they can be categorised according to the environment in which they work.

move:

- ***Ground robots:*** These usually have wheels and can also be classified as humanoid (with two legs) or even resemble animals or insects.
- ***Aerial robots:*** Unmanned aerial vehicles (UAVs).
- ***Underwater robots:*** Known as autonomous underwater robots (AUVs).

In mobile robotics, various solutions have been adopted for movement on solid surfaces such as wheels, rails and legs.

According to Secchi (2008), a mobile robot is characterised by having an intelligence between the operations of perception and action, defining its behaviour and enabling it to reach its programmed objectives.

CHAPTER 4

ARTIFICIAL INTELLIGENCE AND LOGIC APPLIED TO ROBOTICS

With impressive speed, robotics is developing more and more, proving to be a very fertile field for technological innovations in all the areas that make it up.

Artificial intelligence is one of the "key" technologies in all this development, enabling the construction of intelligent robots capable of making decisions in unstructured environments, when faced with new and unexpected situations.

As such, robotics can and should be taken as a starting point for testing techniques for building intelligent artificial intelligence systems, subjecting robot designers to new challenges as robotics expands.

4.1 Application of artificial intelligence in mobile robotics

Mobile robots are characterised by the connection between perception and action operations. These operations define the
The robot's behaviour allows it to achieve its programmed objectives in an uncertain environment. Its degree of autonomy depends on its ability to abstract and convert information received

into orders that are applied to the actions of the locomotion system, guaranteeing the effective fulfilment of its task.

The main characteristics of mobile robots are

- *Perception: The* determination of the relationship between the mobile robot and its working environment through its sensors, together with the ability to perceive, is translated into information, generating global and local maps of the environment according to the variable levels of control.
- *Reasoning:* The mobile robot must be able to decide which actions are required at any given time in order to achieve its objectives. The ability to reason depends on planning precise global trajectories and being able to modify them in the event of unexpected obstacles, allowing it to execute and finalise the objectives it has been asked to achieve.

CHAPTER 5

FINAL CONSIDERATIONS

Artificial intelligence is a field of research that has been improving on an enormous scale in recent years. In addition to robotics, AI is part of many other areas. Today we have neural networks and their learning concepts to go beyond the great innovations of the technological world and apply them in areas where they weren't thought possible.

The field of artificial neural networks and their application in mobile robotics is, above all, extremely vast and promising because it is a subject that has been around for a long time and has now gained a lot of credibility due to new discoveries.

Mobile robots are able to carry out tasks without the constant need for human supervision because they are equipped with various sensors that allow them to perceive the events around them and make intelligent decisions.

Despite all the benefits of applying intelligent systems to robotics, some people still believe that robotics can and automation will wipe out the jobs of countless workers.

However, intelligent mobile robotics is increasingly tending to prevent humans from carrying out difficult and tiring tasks by making programmed decisions, identifying objects and establishing a connection between man and machine in order to improve in various areas.

CHAPTER 6

BIBLIOGRAPHICAL REFERENCES

ARKIN, R. C. Behaviour-Based Robotics. Cambridge: Massachusetts Institute of Technology, 1998. 125p.

CHATILA, R.; GIRALT, G. An Integrated Navigation and Motion Control System for Autonomous Multisensory Mobile Robots. First International Symposium on Robotics Research, S.l., n.1, p.191-214, 1984.

FELDMAN, R. S. Introduction to Psychology. 6. ed. São Paulo: McGraw-Hill Interameticana, 2007. 858p.

FLOREANO, D.; NOLFI, S. Evolutionary Robotics: The Biology, Intelligence and Technology of Self-Organising Machines. 2. ed. Massachusetts: Bradford Book, 2001. 304p.

HEBB, D. O. The Organisation of Behavior. Wiley, New York: McGill University, 1949. 326p.

HECKERMAN, D. E. Probabilistic Similarity Networks. London, England: Massachusetts Institute of Technology, 1991. 263p.

HOPFIELD, J. J. Neural networks and physical systems with emergent collective computational abilities. Proc. Natl. Acad. Sci, USA, v.79, n.1, p.2554-2558, 1982.

MCCARTHY, J. Electronic errors. The electronic errors, Gubern, Darthmouth, v.0, n.1, p.52, 1956.

MCCLELLAND, J. L.; RUMELHART, D. E. Explorations in Parallel Distributed Processing. London: Bradford Book, 1987. 333p.

MCCULLOCH, W. S.; PITTS, W. H. A logical calculus of the ideas immanent in nervous activity. Bulletin of Mathematical Biophysics, University of Oxford, v.5, n.1, p.115-133, 1946. Available at: <www.cse.chalmers.se/~coquand/AUTOMATA/mcp.pdf > Accessed on: 30 Oct. 2016

MINSKY, M. Steps Toward Artificial Intelligence. Proceedings of the ire, London, England, v.January, n.5, p.8-23, 1951.

MORAVEC, Hans Peter. Towards Automatic Visual Obstacle Avoidance. Fifteenth International Join Conference on Artificial Intelligence, Cambridge-MA-USA, n.0, p.584, 1977.

MORAVEC, Hans Peter. Obstacle avoidance and navigation in the real world by a seeing robot rover, PhD in Computer Science, 1980.

NASA, Mars Exploration Rover Launches. NASA: 2003.

NILSSON, N. A Mobile Automaton: An Application of Artificial Intelligence Techniques. International Join Conference on Artificial Intelligence (IJCAI-69), Washington-DC-USA, n.0, p.69, 1969.

SCHAFER, J. B. Hands-on Artificial Intelligence Education Using LEGO Mindstorm. Hands-on Artificial Intelligence Education Using LEGO Mindstorms, University of Northern Iowa, n.1, p.20, 2004. Available in: <www.cs.uni.edu/~schafer/publications/MICS_2004.pdf> Accessed on: 30 Oct. 2016

SHIROMA, Vision Control for Robotic Vehicles. Campinas-SP-Brazil: Gráfica Independente, 2004. 21p.

WIDESOFT, History of Computing. S.l, Web, v.0, n.0, p.Web,

2006.

MIX
Papier aus verantwortungsvollen Quellen
Paper from responsible sources
FSC® C105338

Printed by Books on Demand GmbH, Norderstedt / Germany